DR. EMMET FOX

THE MENTAL EQUIVALENT

THE SECRET OF DEMONSTRATION

THE MENTAL EQUIVALENT

THE SECRET OF DEMONSTRATION

BY
EMMET FOX

ISBN: 978-93-5128-989-0(HB)

First Published in 1943
Indian Reprint in 2017

Published by

Kalpaz Publications
C-30, Satyawati Nagar,
Delhi – 110052
E-mail: kalpaz@hotmail.com
Website: kalpazpublications.com
Ph.: +91-9212142040

CONTENTS

CHAPTER - 1

THE MENTAL EQUIVALENT

This book is the comprised of two lectures delivered by Emmet Fox at Unity School of Christianity, Kansas City, Mo.

We Are all supremely interested in one subject. There is one thing that means more to us than all the other things in the world put together, and that is our search for God and the understanding of His nature. The aim of the metaphysical movement is to teach the practice of the presence of God.

We practice the presence of God by seeing Him everywhere, in all things and in all people, despite any appearances to the contrary. As we look about the world with the eyes of the flesh, we see in-harmony, fear, and all sorts of difficulties; but our leader Jesus Christ taught us, saying, "Judge not according to appearance, but judge righteous judgment." So when we see the appearance of evil we look through it to the truth that lies back of it. As soon as we see this truth, and see it spiritually, the appearance changes, because this is a mental world. NOW most people do not know this: they think it is a material world, and that is why humanity has so many problems. After nineteen centuries of formal Christianity the world is passing through desperate difficulties. But we know the Truth; we do not judge by appearances. We know that we live in a mental world, and to know that is the key to life.

If a child could be taught only one thing, it should be taught that this is a mental world. I would let all the other things go and teach him that.

Whatever enters into your life is but the material expression of some belief in your own mind The kind of body you have, the kind of home you have, the kind of work you do, the kind of people you meet, are all conditioned by and correspond to the mental concepts you are holding. The Bible teaches that from beginning to end. I am putting it in the language of metaphysics; the Bible gives it in the language of religion, but it is the same Truth.

About twenty years ago I coined the phrase "mental equivalent." And now I want to say that for anything that you want in your life – a healthy body, a satisfactory vocation, friends, opportunities, and above all the understanding of God – you must furnish a mental equivalent. Supply yourself with a mental equivalent, and the thing must come to you. Without a mental equivalent it cannot come. Now as to the things in your life that you would like to be rid of, (everyone has such things in his life). Perhaps bodily difficulties or faults of character are the most important. We all have habits of thought and action, and we all have business, family, and personal conditions we would like to be rid of. If we rid our mind of the mental equivalent of them, they must go.

Everything that you see or feel on the material plane, whether it is your body, your home, your business, or your city, is but the expression in the concrete of a mental equivalent held by you. Everything in your city is the embodiment of mental equivalents held by the citizens. Everything in your country is the embodiment of mental equivalents held by the people of the country; and the state of the world embodies the mental equivalent of the two thousand million people who make up the world.

What about war? That is the physical expression of a mental equivalent held by the human race. The human race has believed in the old bogey of fear. It has believed that you can enrich yourself by taking something belonging to someone else. It has believed in death. It has believed in lack. It has believed that aggression pays and that helping yourself to other people's things is a good policy. We have all believed this in some degree. The natural result of this has been to precipitate in the outer a picture of war, death, suffering, and so on. Because humanity had the mental equivalent of war the war came.

Today the world is beginning to get the mental equivalent of peace, and that is why peace will come. A new world will come. The new world will be worth living in. In the great new world that is going to come a little later on – and it will come sooner than some people think – there will be peace, harmony, and understanding between man and man and between nation and nation; but always the thing you see in the outer is the precipitation on the physical plane of a mental equivalent held by one or more people. Now of course I borrowed this expression "mental equivalent" from physics and chemistry. We speak of the mechanical equivalent of heat, for example, and engineers constantly have to work out the equivalent of one kind of energy in another kind of energy. They have to discover how much electricity they will need to do certain mechanical work, such as driving a compressor. They have to find out how much coal will be needed to produce so much electricity, and so on. In like manner there is *a mental equivalent of every object or occurrence on the physical plane.*

The secret of successful living is to build up the mental equivalent that you want; and to get rid of, to expunge, the mental equivalent that you do not want.

Suppose you have rheumatism. I have friends in London who have it all the time; in fact, rheumatism used to be called the national British disease. Some people there have it beginning in October and lasting until March; others only have it until Christmas; others do not get it before Christmas and then have it until February. Of two men living in the same town, doing the same work, eating the same food, drinking the same water, why does one have to have rheumatism from October until February and the other does not have it at all or has it at a different time? Why? Because they have furnished the mental equivalent for what they get. Why is a quarrelsome person always in trouble? He makes New York too hot to hold him, so he goes to Chicago. He thinks he will like it in Chicago; but pretty soon he has enemies in Chicago, so he goes down to Kansas City. He has heard there are nice people there. But soon he is in trouble again. Why? He has what we call a quarrelsome disposition. He has the mental equivalent of strife.

There is another man, and wherever he goes there is peace. If there is a quarrelsome family and he visits them, there is peace while he is there. He has the mental equivalent of peace and true divine love.

So the key to life is to build in the mental equivalents of what you want and to expunge the equivalents of what you do not want. How do you do it? You build in the mental equivalents by thinking quietly, constantly, and persistently of the kind of thing you want, and by thinking that has two qualities: clearness or definiteness, and interest. If you want to build anything into your life – if you want to bring health, right activity, your true place, inspiration; if you want to bring right companionship, and above all if you want understanding of God – form a mental equivalent of the thing which you want by thinking about it a great deal, by thinking clearly and with interest. Remember clarity and interest; those are the two poles.

CHAPTER - 2

UNIVERSAL POLARITY

The Law of polarity is of course a cosmic law. Everything is produced by two other things. Anything that is ever produced anywhere in the universe is produced by two other things. That is the law of polarity. In the organic world we see it as parenthood. In the inorganic world, the world of physics and chemistry, we see it as the protons and electrons. That is how the material universe is built up; it always takes two things to produce a third. And that is the real ultimate meaning back of the Trinity.

There were Trinitarian doctrines before the time of Christ. They had trinities in ancient Egypt and India and in Chaldea and Babylonia – always there is the trinity: father, mother, child: activity, material, production. Go where you like, seek where you will, you find the Trinity.

In the building up of thought the two poles are clarity of thought and warmth of feeling; the knowledge and the feeling. Ninety-nine times in a hundred the reason why metaphysical students do not demonstrate is that they lack the feeling in their treatments. They speak the Truth, oh, yes! "I am divine Spirit. I am one with God." But they do not feel it. The second pole is missing. When they talk about their troubles they are full of feeling, but when they speak of Truth they are about as cold as a dead fish; and I cannot think of anything chillier than a cold fish unless it is a metaphysician who has lost his contact with God. They say, "I am divine Spirit," and they say it with no feeling; but when they say, "I have a terrible pain!" it is loaded with feeling, and so the pain they get and the pain they keep.

A man is out of work and he says: "God is my infinite supply. Man is always in his true place." It is said perfunctorily, with no feeling. But if someone asks him whether he has found work, he says: "I have been out of work two years. I wrote letters. I went after that job, but they were prejudiced against me. They wouldn't give me a chance." As soon as he gets on the negative side, the feeling comes in, and he demonstrates that – he remains unemployed. To think clearly and with feeling leads to demonstration, because you have then built a *mental equivalent.*

Think of the conditions you want to produce. If you want to be healthy, happy, prosperous, doing a constructive work, having a continuous understanding of God, you do not picture it necessarily, but you think it, feel it, and get interested in it. What we call "feeling" in connection with thought is really interest. Feeling is not excitement. Did you ever hear of anything coming from excitement except apoplexy? True "feeling" in thought is *interest.*

You cannot show me any man or woman who is successful in his field, from president down to shoeblack, who is not interested in his work; nor can you show me any man who has his heart in his work who is not successful. The most successful shoeblack you have in town here is vitally interested in his work. He has his heart in it. He is a colored boy, and he loves his work. He did such good work that I gave him an extra tip when he finished polishing my shoes, but no money could really pay him for his work. He was so tickled as he did his work, he loved it so much, that I did not really pay him. He paid himself. He enjoyed it. And he had a line of people waiting for him.

You build a mental equivalent for what you want by getting interested in it. That is the way you create feeling. If you want health, get interested in health. If you want the right place, get interested in service, doing something that is really serving your fellow man.

The reason people do not get ahead in business is that they try to think up schemes to get their fellow men's money instead of thinking up opportunities for service. The successful man gets interested in what he wants to do, and gets rid of things he is not interested in.

How are you going to expunge the wrong mental equivalents? Suppose you have a mental equivalent of resentment, or unemployment, or criticism, or not understanding God. When somebody talks about God, it does not interest you much, you get sleepy or bored. Perhaps you do not get along with people – not that you quarrel with them, but they quarrel with you – the quarrel happens! What is to be done?

The only way to expunge a wrong mental equivalent is to supply the opposite. Think the right thing. The right thought automatically expunges the wrong thought. If you say: "I am not going to think resentment any more. I don't believe in it. There is nothing to it. I am not going to think of it any more," what are you thinking about except resentment? You are still thinking resentment all the time and strengthening the mental equivalent of resentment. Forget it! Think of health and bodily ease and peace and harmony and speak the word for it. Then you are building up a mental equivalent of health. If you want your true place – if your problem is unemployment, no job, the wrong job, or a job you do not like – if you say, "I am not going to think unemployment any more," you are wrong. That is thinking "unemployment," is it not? Think "true place."

If I say to you, "Don't think of the Statue of Liberty in New York," you know what you are thinking about. You are not thinking of anything except the Statue of Liberty. There she is, complete with torch in her hand! I said, "Don't think of her," but you do.

Now I am going to say that some time ago I visited, near Springfield, Illinois, a perfect reproduction of the village of New Salem as it was in the days of Abraham Lincoln. Even the log cabin is furnished as it was in his day. The National Park Commission has done it all.

Now you have forgotten the Statue of Liberty for a few seconds, haven't you? You have been thinking of New Salem. I gave you a different idea. That is the key to the management of your mind, the management of your thinking, and therefore the key to the management of your destiny.

Do not dwell on negative things but replace them, supplant them, with the right, constructive things. The law of mind is that you can only get rid of one thought by substituting another. If a carpenter drives a nail into a wooden wall or into a beam, there it is. Now if he takes a second nail and drives it against the first, the first is driven out and falls on the floor and the second one takes the place of the first one. That is what happens in the mind when you substitute one image for another. For everything in life there has to be a mental equivalent.

If you will start in this very day and refuse to think of your mistakes – and of course that includes the mistakes of other people – if you will cease to think of mistakes and hold the right concepts instead, cease to think fear and think of divine love instead, cease to think lack and think prosperity and the presence of God's abundance instead – and then if you will think as clearly as possible and get interested; you will be building a mental equivalent of happiness and prosperity.

If your thought is very vague, you do not build a mental equivalent. If your thought is lacking in interest, you do not build a mental equivalent. So make your thoughts as clear and definite as possible. Never strain. As soon as you start straining, taking the clenching-the-fist attitude, saying, "I am going to get what I want; I am going to get it if it kills me," all mental building stops.

We have all been told to relax. I have seen people tense up as soon as they were told to relax. They were going to relax if it killed them; and of course they missed the whole point.

Get the thought of what you want as clear as you can. Be definite but not too specific.

If you live in an apartment and say, "I want a house in the country or in the suburbs, and I want it to have a porch and a large yard with trees and flowers," that is all right. But do not say, "I must have a certain house – the one at 257 Ninth Street or 21 Fifth Avenue."

Suppose you go shopping. Well, you should know what you are shopping for. You should have some definite idea. If you say, "I want something, I don't know what – I will leave it to God"; if you say, "I want a business, it may be a farm or a shop I want – I will leave it to Divine Mind," you are foolish. What are you here for? You must have some desires and wishes, because you represent God here. So you must say, "Yes, I want a shop; and I know the kind of shop I want."

I know a woman who demonstrated a hat shop. She had no capital, but she wanted to go into business. She wanted a hat shop. She loves to make hats. She has a natural flair for it. She can make hats that look well on the homeliest people; and this is the art of millinery, isn't it? She was a good businesswoman, so she built the mental equivalent of a hat shop. She did not say, "I must be in a certain block on a certain street." She did not say, "I am going to get a hat shop if it kills me" or "I am going to get a hat shop, and I want Jane Smith's hat shop." She built a definite mental equivalent, and that is the right way. If you say, "I want a strong, healthy body," and build up a mental equivalent for it by constantly thinking of your body as perfect, that is fine. Do not think of details very much. Do not say, "First of all I'm going to get my teeth fixed up with right thought, and I'll let my bald head wait" or "Maybe I should get my bald head fixed up first, because my teeth can wait." It is the details that are wrong. The evil of outlining lies in going into small details and in saying, "I want it in my time, in my way, whether God wants it or not." Apart from that (going too much into small details) you must have definite ideas.

Do not strain to get your ideas clear. They will be clearer the second day or the fifty-second day. If you have a pair of field glasses and you look at something and want the focus clearer, you slowly turn the wheel until the focus is clear.

Getting your mental equivalent may take you a week or a month or a year. *Charge it with interest, like* an electric charge, or it is dead. Love is the only way. You cannot be interested in a thing unless you love it. If you love it, it is filled with interest, it is filled with energy and life, and it comes true.

There is an interesting story about Napoleon. He thought a big nose was a sign of strong character. He said, "Give me a man with plenty of nose." If someone came to him and said that a certain officer ought to be promoted, he would say: "Has he got plenty of nose? Give me a man with a big nose." If an officer was killed, he replaced him with someone with a big nose. You know what happened. The law sent him Wellington, and Wellington destroyed him. Wellington had the largest nose in English history. He said himself it was more of a handle than a nose. Take that as a Tjoke if you like, but it does carry an important lesson.

The doctrine of the mental equivalent is the essence of the metaphysical teaching; the doctrine that you will get whatever you provide the mental equivalent for.

I have known some very, very remarkable cases where people furnished the mental equivalent and out of the blue came things they never could have hoped for in the ordinary way. I know many men and women in London and New York and other places who seemingly had no human chance to attain success; but they got hold of this knowledge of mental equivalents, they quietly and faithfully applied this knowledge; and sometime sooner or later the thing they wanted came to them, without any help from anything outside; and it stayed with them and brought a blessing.

CHAPTER - 3

BUILDING A NEW MENTAL EQUIVALENT

It Is your bounden duty to demonstrate, and in order to do so successfully you need to know why you should do so. Why should you demonstrate at all? Some people say,

"Since God is all, and everything is perfect, why should I seek to demonstrate His law?" Because you have to prove the harmony of being in your own life. That is why. If there were no need to demonstrate, one might just as well go to bed and stay there or, more simply still, stroll around to the nearest undertaker.

Of course we are here on earth to express God, and true expression is what we call demonstration, because it demonstrates the law of Being. It is your duty to be healthy, prosperous, and free. It is your duty to express God to the utmost of your power; and you have no right to relinquish your efforts until you have accomplished this. Until you have excellent health and are visibly regenerating, until you have found your true place and right activity, until you are free from conscious fear, anxiety, and criticism, you are not demonstrating, and you must find out why and correct the error, whatever it is.

Jesus has told us that we always demonstrate our consciousness, and Unity is teaching the same truth today. You always demonstrate what you habitually have in your mind. What sort of mind have you? I am not going to tell you – and do not let anyone else tell you either, because they do not know. People who like you will think your mentality is better than it is; those who do not like you will think it is worse. So do not ask anybody about your mentality; but examine your conditions and see what you are demonstrating. This method is scientific and infallible.

If an automobile engineer is working out a new design for an engine, if he is going to do something different about the valves, for instance, he doesn't say: "I wonder what Smith thinks about this. I like Smith. If Smith is against this I won't try it." Nor does he say, "I won't try this idea because it comes from France, and I don't like those people." He is impersonal and perfectly unemotional about it. He says, "I will test it out, and decide by the results I obtain."

Then he tries it out, measuring the results carefully, and decides accordingly. He does not laugh, or cry, or get excited, or bang the table; but he tests out the idea scientifically and judges only by results.

That is how you should handle your mentality. That is how you should practice the metaphysical teaching. You demonstrate the state of your mind at any given time. You experience in the outer what you really think in the inner. This is the meaning of the old saying "As within so without." Note carefully that in the Bible the word "withip" always means thought and the word "without" means manifestation or experience. That is why Jesus said that the kingdom of heaven (health, harmony, and freedom) is within. Harmonious thought means harmonious experience. Fear thought or anger thought means suffering or frustration.

This brings me to the most important thing I want to say, namely that if you want to change your life; if you want to be healthier, happier, younger, more prosperous; above all, if you want to get nearer to God – and I know that you do – *you must change your thought and keep it changed.* That is the secret of controlling your life, and there is no other way. Jesus Himself could not have done it in any other way, because this is a cosmic law. Change your thought and keep it changed. We have all been taught this very thing since the metaphysical movement began. I heard it stated in those very words many times nearly forty years ago in London; but most of us are slow to realize the importance of it. If you want to change some condition in your life, you must change your thought about it and keep it changed. Then the condition will change accordingly. All that anyone else can do for you is to help you change your thought. That is what a metaphysician can do for you, but you yourself must keep it changed. No one else can think for you. "No man can save his brother's soul or pay his brother's debt."

To change your thought and keep it changed is the way to build a new mental equivalent; it is the secret of accomplishment. You already have a mental equivalent for everything that is in your life today; and you must destroy the patterns for the things you do not want, and then they will disappear. You must build a new pattern or mental equivalent for the things you want, and then they will come into your life.

Of course changing your thought for a short time is the easiest thing in the world. Everyone does this when he goes to a metaphysical meeting. The beautiful atmosphere and the positive instruction make people feel optimistic. The teacher reminds the audience of the Truth of Being, and they think, "I believe that, and I am going to practice it." But five minutes after they have left the meeting they forget about it, perhaps for hours. The trouble with most students is not that they do not change their thought but that they do not keep it changed.

If you want health you must cease to think sickness and fear, and you must get the habit of thinking health and harmony. There can be no sickness without fear. You cannot be adversely affected by anything if you really have no fear concerning it. Everyone has many fears in the subconscious mind that he is not consciously aware of, but they are operating just the same.

A man said: "I entered a town in a foreign country in the east of Europe during a typhoid epidemic. I did not know there was any typhoid. I never thought about it. I didn't know the language and couldn't read the papers. They were printed in Greek. Yet I got typhoid and had quite a siege. How do you account for that?"

The explanation is that he believed in typhoid fever. He believed one an catch it from others, and that it makes one very ill, for so many days, and therefore he had a subconscious fear of it. He subconsciously knew there was typhoid around, and as it always does, the subconscious enacted or dramatized his real beliefs and fears, and presented him with a good hearty case of typhoid.

If he had really believed that he was a child of God who could not be hurt by anything, he would not have had typhoid.

Change your thought and keep it changed, not for ten seconds or even ten days but steadily and permanently. Then you will build a new mental equivalent, and *a mental equivalent is always demonstrated.*

The secret of harmony and success is to concentrate your thought upon harmony and success. That is why I teach that attention is the key to life. What you attend to or concentrate upon you bring into your life, because you are building a mental equivalent.

Many people fail to concentrate successfully because they think that concentration means will power. They actually try to concentrate with their muscles and blood vessels. They frown. They clench their hands. Unwittingly they are thinking of an engineer's drill or a carpenter's bit and brace. They suppose that the harder you press the faster you get through. But all this is quite wrong.

Forget the drill and think of a photographic camera. In a camera there is of course no question of pressure. There the secret lies in focus. If you want to photograph something you focus your camera lens quietly, steadily, and persistently on it for the necessary length of time. Suppose I want to photograph a vase of flowers. What do I do? Well, I do not press it violently against the lens of the camera. That would be silly. I place the vase in front of the camera and keep it there. But suppose that after a few moments I snatch away the vase and hold a book in front of the camera, and then snatch that away, and hold up a chair, and then put the flowers back for a few moments, and so forth. You know what will happen to my photograph. It will be a crazy blur. Is not that what people do to their minds when they cannot keep their thoughts concentrated for any length of time? They think health for a few minutes and then they think sickness or fear. They think prosperity and then they think depression. They think about bodily perfection and then they think about old age and their pains and aches. Is it any wonder that man is so apt to demonstrate the "marred image?"

Note carefully that I did not advocate taking one thought and trying to hold it by will power. That is bad. You must allow a train of relevant thoughts to have free play in your mind, one leading naturally to the next, but they must all be positive, constructive, and harmonious, and appertaining to your desire; and you must think quietly and without effort. Then you will get the mental equivalent of all-round success, and then success itself will follow; success in health, in social relationships, in your work, in your spiritual development.

CHAPTER - 4

MAINTAINING THE NEW EQUIVALENT

It Is always good to make a practical experiment, so I advise you to take a single problem in your life – something you want to get rid of or something you want to obtain – and change your thought about this thing, and keep it changed. Do not be in a hurry to select your problem; take your time.

Do not tell anyone you are doing this. If you tell a friend about it you are thereby strongly affirming the existence of the problem, which is the very thing you are trying to get rid of. If you tell your friend that you are going to work on your rheumatism or on lack, you are making these things very real to your subconscious mind. Also your spiritual energy is leaking away, as electricity does in what we call a "ground?'

Take your problem and change your mind concerning it, and keep it changed for a month, and you will be astonished at the results you will get. If you really do keep your thought changed you will not have to wait a month. If you really change your thought and keep it changed, the demonstration may come in a few hours. But to keep tensely looking for the demonstration is really affirming the existence of the problem, is it not? The secret is to keep your thought changed into the new condition. So keep your thought carefully, quietly expressive of the new condition that you want to produce. Believe what you are thinking, and to prove that you believe it you must act the part.

By changing your mind about your problem in this way and keeping it changed, you are building a new mental equivalent, a mental equivalent of harmony and success, and that mental equivalent, as we know, must be outpictured in your experience.

For a while you will find that your thought will keep slipping back into the old rut. Such is the force of habit. But if you are quietly persistent you will ain the victory. It is always a little difficult to change a habit, but it can be done, and then the new right habit becomes easier than the old wrong habit, and that is how a new mental equivalent is built.

Change your mind and keep it changed.

Do not talk about the negative thing or act as if it were there. Act your part as though the new condition were already in being in the outer. If you will do this, the new condition will presently appear in the outer, because the outer is always but the projection or outpicturing of the inner.

We project our own belief and call it experience, and this gives us the clue to the difference between a true action and a false or unreal action.

What is true action? A true action is one that really changes things, that gets you somewhere. A false action does not. For example, if your car has traction it is moving. That is a true action, and you will presently reach your destination; but if it does not have traction there will be movement, vibration, but you will not get anywhere. You are wearing out the engine and perhaps the tires, but you do not get anywhere. The same thing happens when a soldier is "marking time" as we say. He is tiring himself and wearing out his shoes but not getting anywhere. These are examples of false action.

Suppose you have a difficult letter to write or a sermon or a lecture to prepare. Suppose you sit in front of a sheet of paper and draw curlicues or cut the pencil to pieces or tear your hair. These would be false actions, and many people do just that. Such actions get you nowhere. To decide what you are going to say, to start a current of thought and then write it down, is true action. You will note that the difference is that in the false action you begin from the outside. You had not prepared your thoughts. You tried to begin by writing. With the true action you got your thoughts in order first and then the writing or outer activity followed. A false action means deadlock; a true action is always fruitful.

True activity is always from within outward. False activity tries to work from without inward. One is centrifugal and the other centripetal, if you want to be technical. If you are working from within out, your work is alive and will be productive. If you are working from outside inward, your work is dead, and it will have a bad effect on you.

Artists and literary people speak of "potboilers." You know what a potboiler is. It is a picture that you paint or a story that you write, not because you are interested but just to keep the monetary returns coming in. It is never good, because it is not the result of inspiration. It is done from the outside and is a false action. It is a common saying among writers that three potboilers will kill any talent; and that is true. The proper way to paint a picture is to see beauty somewhere, in a landscape or in a beautiful face, or wherever you please. You thrill to that beauty, and then you go to the canvas and express your inspiration there. That is art, and that is true action. It inspires other people and it helps and develops you yourself.

If you write a story or a novel because you have observed life, because you have seen certain things happen and studied certain people, and write it all down because you are alive with it, that is a true action and you write a great book. Dickens, George Eliot, Balzac, and all the great authors wrote in that way. But if you say, "I will do fifteen hundred words a day and give my publishers the 'mixture as before' and that will secure my income," your work will be dead. And this policy will kill any talent that you may have.

If you are in business and you are interested in your job and love it, your work is a positive action and must ultimately bring you success. Even if the work is uncongenial but nevertheless you say, "This is my job for the moment; I am going to do it as well as I can, and then something better will open up," you are working from within outward. Your work is a positive action, and before long something really congenial will come to you.

Most people know that these things are true. They know that they are true for pictures and stories and business life, but they do not realize that they are equally true for the things of the soul. Yet such is the case. If you pray and meditate from the outside just because you think it is a duty or because you will feel guilty if you do not, your prayers will be dead. You will get no demonstration and make no spiritual progress, and you will get no joy. But if you feel that when you are praying and meditating you are visiting with God, and that these moments are the happiest in the twentyfour hours, then you are working from within outward. Your spiritual growth will be fruitful, and you will grow very rapidly in spiritual understanding. When you pray in this way there is no strain and your soul is filled with peace.

The great enemy of prayer is a sense of tension. When you are tense you are always working from the outside inward. Tension in prayer is probably the greatest cause of failure to demonstrate. Remember that the mind always stops working when you are tense. When you think, "I must demonstrate this" or "I must get that in three days," you are tense; you are using your will power, and you will do more harm than good.

Remember this: The door of the soul opens inward. If you will remember this it will save you years and years of waiting for demonstrations. Write in your notebook, the one you carry in your pocket – not the notebook you keep locked in your desk, because that is a mausoleum – or better still, write it on a card, and place it on your dresser: "The door of the soul opens inward." And pray to God that you may remember that truth every time you turn to Him in prayer. You know what it means when a door opens inward: the harder you push against it the tighter you close it. When you press or force or hurl yourself against it you only close it on yourself. When you relax and draw back, you give it a chance to open. In all theaters and other public buildings the doors open outward. The law insists upon this because crowds are apt to become panic-stricken and then they push, and if the doors opened inward the people would imprison themselves and be killed. The door of the soul opens inward!

That is the law. Relax mentally, draw away from your problem spiritually, and the action of God will open the door for you and you will be free.

There is an old legend of the Middle Ages that is very instructive. It seems that a citizen was arrested by one of the Barons and shut up in a dungeon in his castle. He was taken down dark stairs, down, down, down, by a ferocious-looking jailer who carried a great key a foot long. The door of a cell was opened, and he was thrust into a dark hole. The door shut with a bang, and there he was.

He lay in that dark dungeon for twenty years. Each day the jailer would come, the big door would be opened with a great creaking and groaning, a pitcher of water and a loaf of bread would be thrust in and the door closed again.

Well, after twenty years the prisoner decided that he could not stand it any longer. He wanted to die but he did not want to commit suicide, so he decided that the next day when the jailer came he would attack him. The jailer would then kill him in self-defense, and thus his misery would be at an end. He thought he would examine the door carefully so as to be ready for tomorrow and, going over, he caught the handle and turned it. To his amazement the door opened, and upon investigation he found that there was no lock upon it and never had been, and that for all those twenty years he had not been locked in, except in belief.

At any time in that period he could have opened the door if only he had known it. He thought it was locked, but it was not. He groped along the corridor and felt his way upstairs. At the top of the stairs two soldiers were chatting, and they made no attempt to stop him. He crossed the great yard without attracting attention. There was an armed guard on the drawbridge at the great gate, but they paid no attention to him, and he walked out a free man.

He went home unmolested and lived happily ever after. He could have done this any time through those long years since his arrest if he had known enough, but he did not. He was a captive, not of stone and iron but of false belief. He was not locked in; he only thought he was. Of course this is only a legend, but it is an extremely instructive one.

We are all living in some kind of prison, some of us in one kind, some in another; some in a prison of lack, some in a prison of remorse and resentment, some in a prison of blind, unintelligent fear, some in a prison of sickness. But always the prison is in our thought and not in the nature of things.

There is no truth in our seeming troubles. There is no reality in lack. There is no power in time or conditions to make us old or tired or sick.

The Jesus Christ teaching, and the Unity movement in particular, comes to us and says: You are not locked in a prison of circumstances. You are not chained in any dungeon. In the name of God, turn the handle, walk out, and be free."

Build a mental equivalent of freedom, of vibrant physical health, of true prosperity, of increasing understanding and achievement for God. Build it by thinking of it, having faith in it and acting the part, and the old limitation equivalent will gradually fade out, for the door is unlocked and the voice of God in your heart says, "Be free."